TRINITY
COLLEGE LONDON PRESS

GRADE

01

BASS

Published by
Trinity College London Press Ltd.
trinitycollege.com

Registered in England
Company no. 09726123

Photography by Zute Lightfoot, lightfootphoto.com

Printed in England by Caligraving Ltd.

THE EXAM AT A GLANCE

In your exam you will perform a set of three songs and one of the session skills assessments. You can choose the order of your set list.

SONG 1

Choose a song from this book.

SONG 2

Choose *either* a different song from this book
or a song from the list of additional Trinity Rock & Pop arrangements, available at trinityrock.com
or a song you have chosen yourself: this could be your own cover version or a song that you have written. It should be at the same level as the songs in this book and match the parameters at trinityrock.com

SONG 3: TECHNICAL FOCUS

Song 3 is designed to help you develop specific and relevant techniques in performance. Choose one of the technical focus songs from this book, which cover two specific technical elements.

SESSION SKILLS

Choose *either* **playback** *or* **improvising**.

Session skills are an essential part of every Rock & Pop exam. They are designed to help you develop the techniques music industry performers need.

Sample tests are available in our *Session Skills* books and free examples can be downloaded from trinityrock.com

ACCESS ALL AREAS

GET THE FULL ROCK & POP EXPERIENCE ONLINE AT TRINITYROCK.COM

We have created a range of digital resources to support your learning and give you insider information from the music industry, available online.
You will find support, advice and digital content on:

- Songs, performance and technique
- Session skills
- The music industry

You can access tips and tricks from industry professionals featuring:

- Bite-sized videos that include tips from professional musicians on techniques used in the songs
- 'Producer's notes' on the tracks, to increase your knowledge of rock and pop
- Blog posts on performance tips, musical styles, developing technique and advice from the music industry

JOIN US ONLINE AT:

 /TRINITYROCKANDPOP   @TRINITY_ROCK   ▶ /TRINITYROCKANDPOP   and at **TRINITYROCK.COM**

CONTENTS

THE AUDIO

Professional demo & backing tracks can be downloaded free, see inside cover for details.

Music preparation and book layout by Andrew Skirrow for Camden Music Services
Music consultants: Nick Crispin, Chris Walters, Christopher Hussey, Mike Mansbridge
Audio arranged, recorded & produced by Tom Fleming
Bass arrangements by Sam Burgess & Ben Heartland

Musicians
Bass: Ben Heartland
Drums: George Double
Guitar: Tom Fleming
Cello: Sophie Gledhill
Vocals: Bo Walton, Brendan Reilly, Emily Barden

YOUR
PAGE
NOTES

01 GRADE

BASS

TECHNICAL FOCUS

BILLIE JEAN

MICHAEL JACKSON

WORDS AND MUSIC: MICHAEL JACKSON

SINGLE BY
Michael Jackson

ALBUM
Thriller

B-SIDE
It's the Falling in Love

RELEASED
2 January 1983

RECORDED
**1982
Westlake Recording
Studios
Los Angeles
California, USA**

LABEL
Epic

WRITER
Michael Jackson

PRODUCERS
**Quincy Jones
Michael Jackson**

The self-proclaimed King of Pop, Michael Jackson was a star from the age of 11, when the Jackson Five scored No. 1 hits in the US with their first four singles in 1970. He began his solo career a year later and, with the release of 1982's *Thriller*, would break the world record for the best-selling album in history.

'Billie Jean' was the second single from *Thriller*, released a month after the album in January 1983 and going on to top the US and UK singles charts two months later. Its accompanying video was the first by a solo black artist to be given heavy rotation on MTV, and only after it had reached No. 1. Jackson memorably performed the song on the *Motown 25: Yesterday, Today, Forever* TV special, broadcast in May that year to more than 50 million people, during which he unveiled what would become his signature dance move, the moonwalk. Both the single and the album picked up numerous awards, including an unprecedented eight Grammy Awards and eight American Music Awards.

TECHNICAL FOCUS

Two technical focus elements are featured in this song:

- Articulation
- Coordination

Articulation is important in this song. You'll need to make a clear contrast between the separate, almost jerky quavers at the start and the smooth, melodic material at the pre-chorus. **Coordination** is a challenge at the opening and whenever the opening material comes back, so aim for neat fingerwork to help the hands align.

TECHNICAL FOCUS

BILLIE JEAN

WORDS AND MUSIC: MICHAEL JACKSON

Pop ♩ = 108 (2 bars count-in)

Verse

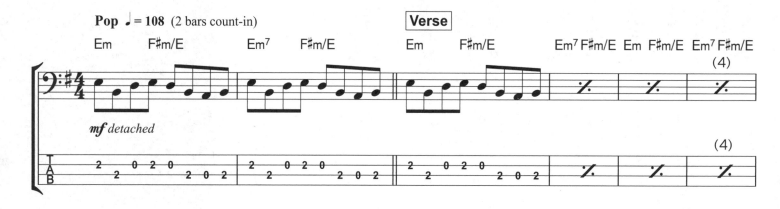

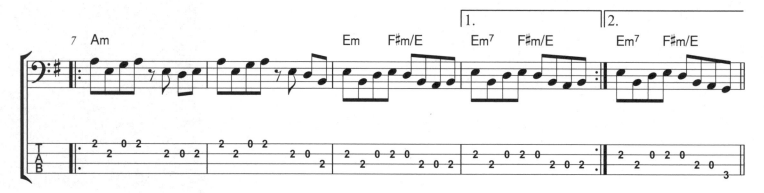

Pre-chorus

People always told me...

legato

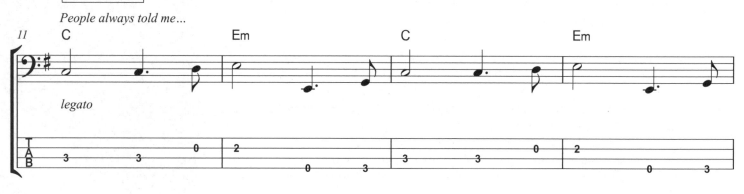

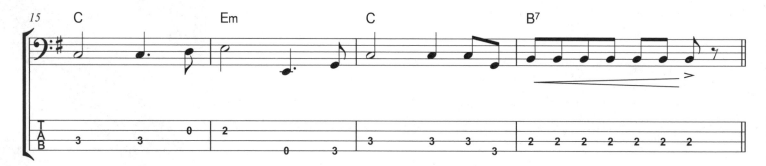

Chorus

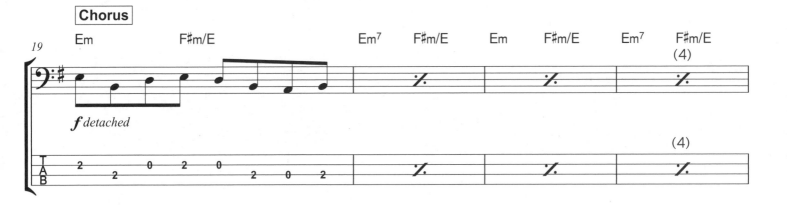

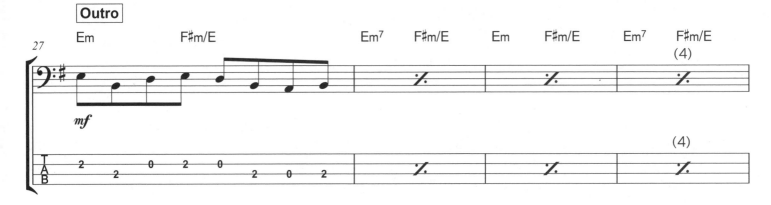

Outro

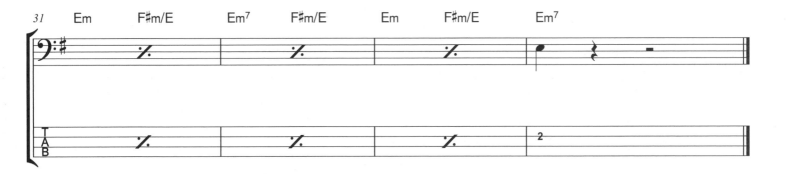

YOUR
PAGE
NOTES

FLOAT ON
MODEST MOUSE

**WORDS AND MUSIC: ISAAC BROCK, DANN GALLUCCI, ERIC JUDY
BENJAMIN WEIKEL**

SINGLE BY
Modest Mouse

ALBUM
**Good News for People Who
Love Bad News**

B-SIDE
I've Got it All (Most)

RELEASED
14 February 2004

RECORDED
**September-October 2003
Sweet Tea Studio
Oxford, Mississippi, USA**

**Easley Recording
Memphis, Tennessee
USA (album)**

LABEL
Epic

WRITERS
**Isaac Brock
Dann Gallucci
Eric Judy
Benjamin Weikel**

PRODUCER
Dennis Herring

Modest Mouse have been going since 1992, formed by Isaac Brock (vocals/guitar), Eric Judy (bass) and Jeremiah Green (drums) in Washington, Seattle. Former collaborator Dann Gallucci joined the band on guitar for their fourth album, the 2004 commercial breakthrough *Good News for People Who Love Bad News*.

Frontman Isaac Brock was inspired to write 'Float On', an ode to looking at the bright side in the face of disaster, following the death of two close friends and the temporary departure of Green from the band following a nervous breakdown. To a stomping rhythm, the song details a number of mishaps which are offset by the positive message of the chorus. The song's slow-burning success helped *Good News for People Who Like Bad News* sell over 1.5 million copies in the US alone, and 'Float On' topped the Billboard Modern Rock Tracks chart almost six months after its initial release. Catchy, humorous and optimistic, it has become the band's signature song and was nominated for a Grammy Award for Best Rock Song in 2005.

 **PERFORMANCE TIPS**

This song features a lot of repeated crotchets for the bass, and you'll need to find exactly the right amount of separation between these to capture the gently driving feel of the original version. You'll also need to place each crotchet precisely on the beat. The chorus features some sustained dotted minims, which should be held for their full length.

FLOAT ON

WORDS AND MUSIC:
ISAAC BROCK, DANN GALLUCCI,
ERIC JUDY, BENJAMIN WEIKEL

Verse

Indie Rock ♩=101 (2 bars count-in)

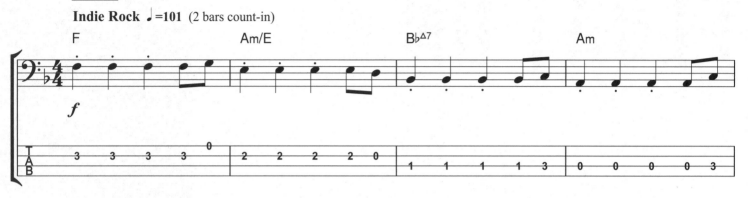

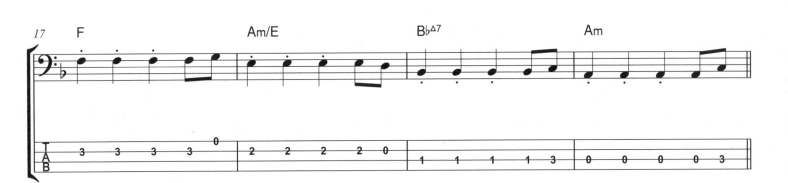

Chorus

YOUR
PAGE
NOTES

TECHNICAL FOCUS

JUST LOOKING
STEREOPHONICS

WORDS AND MUSIC: KELLY JONES

SINGLE BY
Stereophonics

ALBUM
Performance & Cocktails

B-SIDE
**Postmen Do Not Great
Movie Heroes Make**

Sunny Afternoon

RELEASED
22 February 1999

RECORDED
1995-1998

**Real World Studios, Bath
Somerset, England**

**Parkgate Studios, Battle
East Sussex, England**

**Rockfield Studios
Monmouthshire, Wales
(album)**

LABEL
V2 Records

WRITER
Kelly Jones

PRODUCERS
**Steve Bush
Marshall Bird**

Hailing from a village in south-west Wales, Stereophonics formed in 1992 and are led by singer, guitarist and songwriter Kelly Jones. Six of the band's nine studio albums have topped the UK charts and ten of their singles have reached the top five.

'Just Looking' was released ahead of Stereophonics' second album, 1999's *Performance and Cocktails*, propelling the album to No. 1 in the UK. The band celebrated this success on 31 July that year with a headline show at the 50,000-capacity Morfa Stadium in Swansea, shortly before it was demolished. A month later the band won Best Album and Best British Band honours at the Kerrang! Awards, and it went on to sell over 2.5 million copies. In 2007 Stereophonics became only the eighth band to score five consecutive No. 1 albums in the UK, the previous seven being The Beatles, Led Zeppelin, ABBA, Genesis, Oasis, Blur and U2.

TECHNICAL FOCUS

Two technical focus elements are featured in this song:

- Accented syncopation
- Dynamics

The signature riff of this song appears at the chorus, where the bass plays an **accented**, **syncopated** motif. You'll need to play with complete precision and a hard accent on the two notes where this is written. There is also a wide range of **dynamics** to observe, including an unexpected *subito p* at bar 25. These are important for the drama of the song, so aim for maximum contrast between soft and loud.

JUST LOOKING

WORDS AND MUSIC: KELLY JONES

Intro

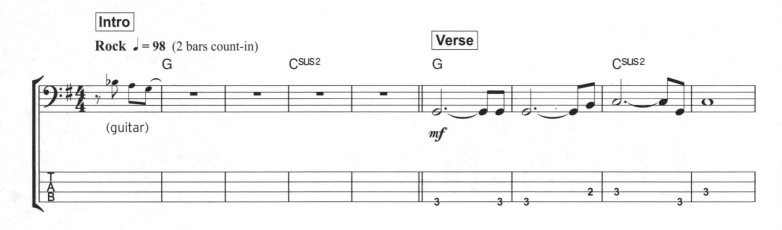

Verse

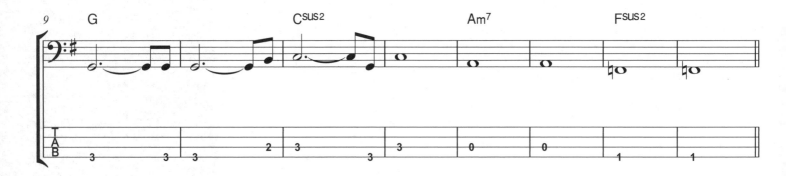

Chorus

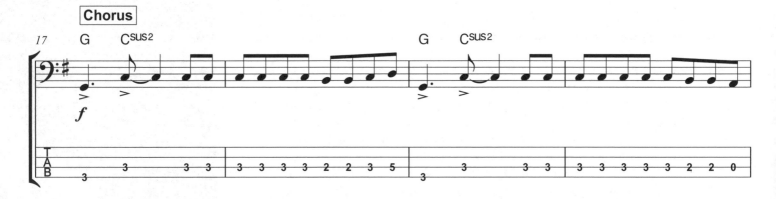

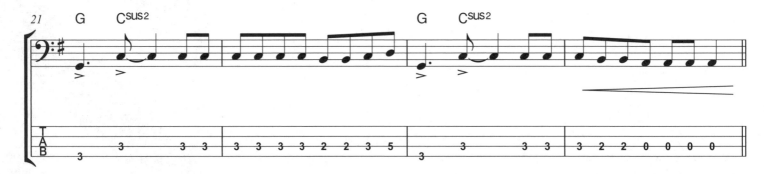

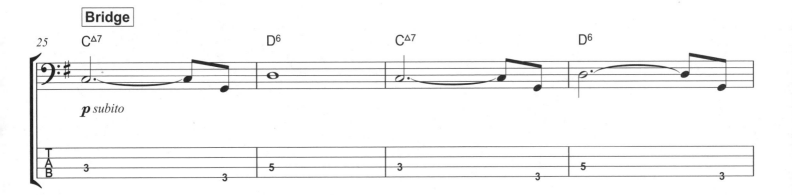

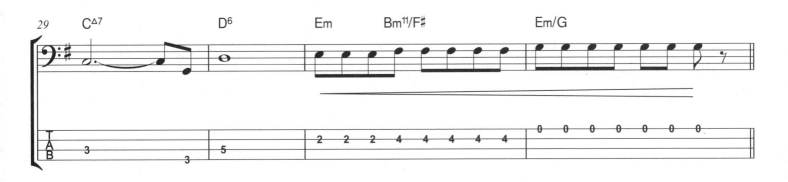

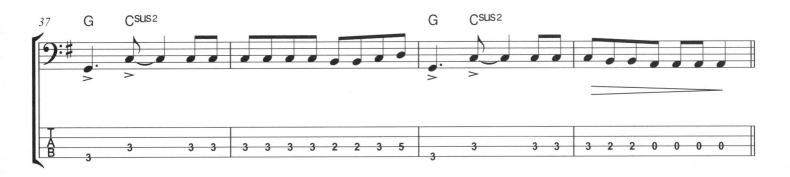

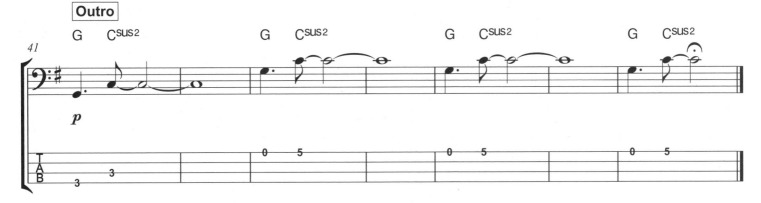

YOUR
PAGE
NOTES

LEARN TO FLY FOO FIGHTERS

WORDS AND MUSIC: DAVE GROHL, NATE MENDEL, TAYLOR HAWKINS

SINGLE BY
Foo Fighters

ALBUM
**There is Nothing
Left to Lose**

B-SIDE
Have a Cigar

RELEASED
18 September 1999

RECORDED
March-June 1999

**Studio 606, Alexandria
Virginia, USA**

**Conway Recording
Studios, Los Angeles
California, USA**

LABEL
**Roswell
RCA**

WRITER(S)
**Dave Grohl
Nate Mendel
Taylor Hawkins**

Initially founded by Nirvana drummer Dave Grohl in 1994 as a solo project following the death of Kurt Cobain, Foo Fighters would grow to include Pat Smear (guitar), Nate Mendel (bass), Taylor Hawkins (drums) and Chris Shiflett (guitar). With Grohl as frontman and guitarist, the band have become one of the 21st century's biggest rock bands worldwide.

'Learn to Fly' was released as the lead single from the Foo Fighters' third album, 1999's *There is Nothing Left to Lose*. Although the band had scored a number of hits worldwide before this, 'Learn to Fly' marked their first top 20 hit in the US, helped in some part by the comic, Grammy Award-winning video. On 30 July 2015, a video was published on YouTube featuring hundreds of singers, guitarists, bassists and drummers performing the song in Cesena, northern Italy. Named Rockin'1000, they sent a plea to the band to come and play a show in their city. The band duly honoured the request, performing there on 3 November 2015 and opening with the song that the 1,000 musicians had played in their honour three months earlier.

⚡ PERFORMANCE TIPS

This rhythmically driving song requires accuracy and commitment from the bass. Whether you are playing the syncopated rhythm of the opening, the sustained semibreves of the chorus or the repeated quavers of bars 17-21, you'll need a high level of precision and an awareness of how this song builds, which is reflected in the written dynamics. The last two bars offer a final challenge for accuracy.

LEARN TO FLY

WORDS AND MUSIC:
DAVE GROHL, NATE MENDEL, TAYLOR HAWKINS

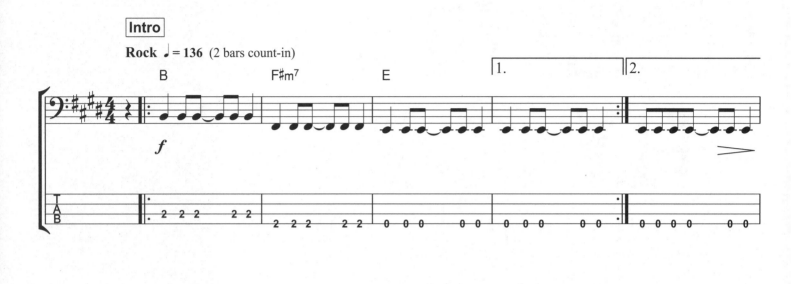

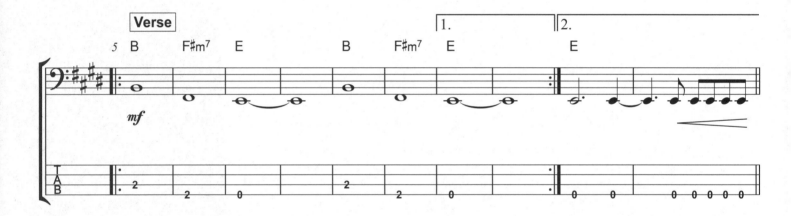

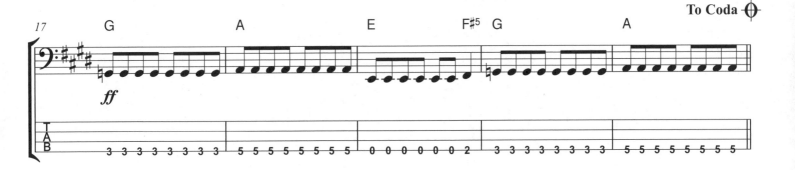

Bridge

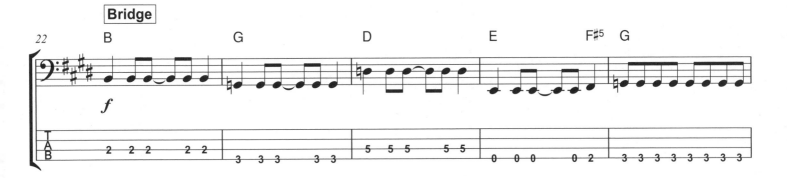

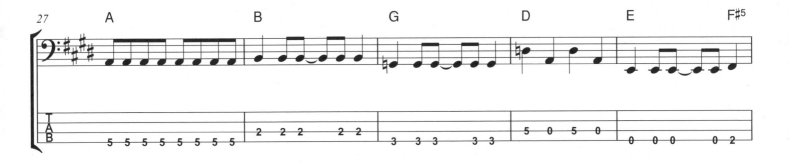

D.S. al Coda
(with repeats)

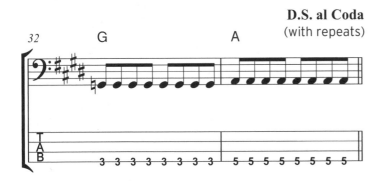

Coda

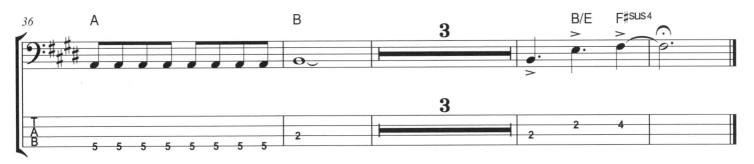

YOUR
PAGE
NOTES

TECHNICAL FOCUS

LABELLED WITH LOVE

SQUEEZE

WORDS AND MUSIC: GLENN TILBROOK, CHRIS DIFFORD

SINGLE BY
Squeeze

ALBUM
East Side Story

B-SIDE
Squabs on Forty Fab

RELEASED
15 May 1981 (album)
25 September 1981 (single)

RECORDED
1980, Eden Studios Chiswick, London England (album)

LABEL
A&M

WRITERS
Glenn Tilbrook Chris Difford

PRODUCERS
Roger Bechirian Elvis Costello

Named after the final album by the Velvet Underground and formed by singer-songwriters Chris Difford and Glenn Tilbrook in 1974, Squeeze earned their credentials on the south-east London pub rock circuit at the same time as fellow Deptford-based band Dire Straits were making their name.

A country-flavoured lament, 'Labelled with Love' was the third single to be released from Squeeze's fourth album, 1981's *East Side Story*, co-produced by Elvis Costello and the band's first album to reach the top 20 in the UK. 'Labelled with Love' became their third and final top-five hit after 'Cool for Cats' and 'Up the Junction'. A narrative-driven song about the end of a relationship after the war, it was inspired by American soldiers in Britain during the second world war who married English girls and took them back to the US. 'Labelled with Love' also provided Difford and Tilbrook with the title for a musical based on their songs which opened two years later.

TECHNICAL FOCUS

Two technical focus elements are featured in this song:

- Swing
- Note lengths

This song has a **swing** feel, and the bass plays an important role in creating this. The quavers in particular should embody the relaxed swing. You'll also need to make sure that the $\frac{2}{4}$ bar does not interrupt the flow. **Note lengths** are also important in this song, and you'll need to take care to observe the quaver rests that appear in each bar.

LABELLED WITH LOVE

WORDS AND MUSIC:
GLENN TILBROOK, CHRIS DIFFORD

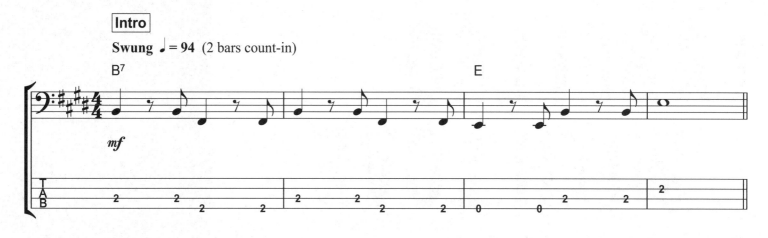

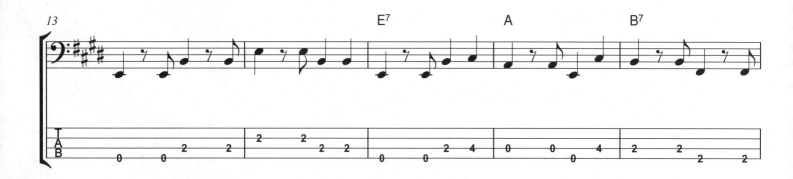

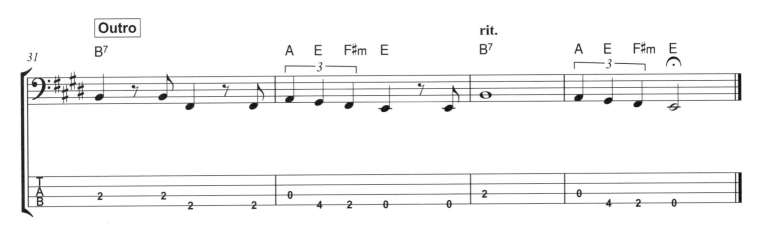

YOUR
PAGE
NOTES

LITTLE TALKS
OF MONSTERS AND MEN

WORDS AND MUSIC: NANNA BRYNDÍS HILMARSDÓTTIR, RAGNAR ÞÓRHALLSSON

SINGLE BY
Of Monsters and Men

ALBUM
My Head is an Animal

B-SIDE
**Six Weeks
Love Love Love
From Finner**

RELEASED
**20 September 2011
(album)
20 December 2011
(single)**

RECORDED
**26-28 March 2011
9-25 January 2012
Studio Syrland
Vatnagarðar, Reykjavík**

LABEL
Universal Republic

WRITERS
**Nanna Bryndís
Hilmarsdóttir
Ragnar Þórhallsson**

PRODUCER(S)
**Of Monsters And Men
Aron Þór Arnarsson**

Of Monsters and Men are a five-piece folk-pop group from Reykjavik, Iceland, fronted by singer-guitarist-songwriters Nanna Bryndís Hilmarsdóttir and Ragnar 'Raggi' Þórhallsson. Their first two albums are 2011's *My Head is an Animal* and 2015's *Beneath the Skin*.

This debut single by Of Monsters and Men proved to be a sizeable international hit after topping the charts in their native Iceland in 2011, reaching No. 1 the following year in Ireland and the top 20 in many other countries (the UK, US, Australia and most of Europe included). Influenced by Bon Iver and Arcade Fire, the band combine a folk, Americana feel with an epic pop sound. Raggi and Nanna were inspired to write 'Little Talks' by an old couple who had lived in Nanna's house for 30 years, and the song is an imaginary conversation between a husband and wife after he has passed away and left her living alone. Though lyrically dark, this catchy song helped propel the album *My Head is an Animal* to sell over a million copies in the US alone.

⚡ PERFORMANCE TIPS

This song is full of contrasts. At the start you'll need to count carefully to lock into the syncopated rhythm, which soon gives way to the verse. Here you are required to count six bars' rest before playing again at bar 17. Be sure to come in precisely on the first beat when bar 17 comes along. Bars 23-24 feature a crescendo over repeated accented quavers, and you'll need to spread the crescendo evenly over the two bars.

LITTLE TALKS

WORDS AND MUSIC:
NANNA BRYNDÍS HILMARSDÓTTIR,
RAGNAR ÞÓRHALLSSON

Intro

Indie Pop ♩ = 104 (2 bars count-in)

Verse

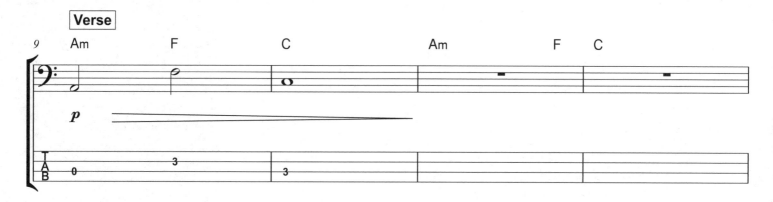

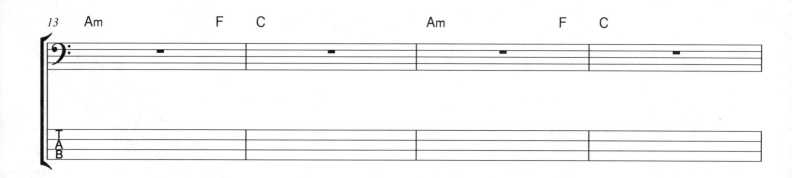

YOUR
PAGE
NOTES

MULL OF KINTYRE

PAUL MCCARTNEY & WINGS

WORDS AND MUSIC: PAUL MCCARTNEY, DENNY LAINE

SINGLE BY
Paul McCartney & Wings

B-SIDE
Girls' School

RELEASED
11 November 1977

RECORDED
9 August 1977

LABEL
EMI

WRITERS
**Paul McCartney
Denny Laine**

PRODUCER
Paul McCartney

Paul McCartney's band Wings emerged a year after The Beatles' 1970 split. The core members were McCartney, his wife Linda and former guitarist of the Moody Blues, Denny Laine. They released seven albums between 1971 and 1979, four of which were chart-toppers in the US.

An unconventional classic, 'Mull of Kintyre' is an anthemic, acoustic waltz, complete with bagpipes and inspired by the southern tip of the Kintyre peninsula in western Scotland. Released as a non-album single in November 1977, the song climbed to No. 1 the UK in its second week of release and remained there for nine weeks. It became the first single to sell over two million copies in the UK, at the time eclipsing The Beatles' 'She Loves You' as the UK's best-selling single ever. It remains the UK's best-selling non-charity single – only 'Candle in the Wind 1997', 'Do They Know It's Christmas?' and 'Bohemian Rhapsody' have outsold it, all for charitable causes.

⚡ PERFORMANCE TIPS

This waltz-time song is stylistically quite different to most rock and pop music. You'll need to capture the lilting rhythm by feeling three beats in each bar and putting a mild emphasis on the first beat. In some places the bass line is a melody all of its own – for example bars 6-7 and 31-32 – so play these sections smoothly, with a sense of leading to the next bar. There's also a key change at bar 24 to look out for.

MULL OF KINTYRE

WORDS AND MUSIC:
PAUL MCCARTNEY, DENNY LAINE

Far have I travelled...

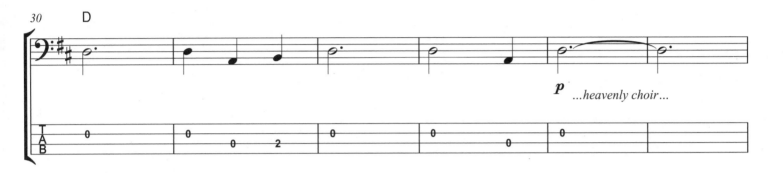

...heavenly choir...

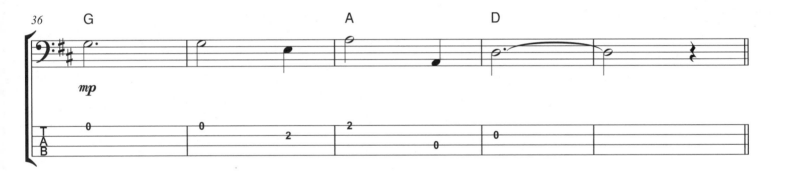

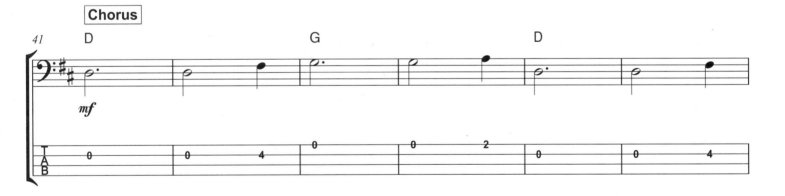

YOUR
PAGE
NOTES

NOT THE GIRL YOU THINK YOU ARE CROWDED HOUSE

WORDS AND MUSIC: NEIL FINN

SINGLE BY
Crowded House

ALBUM
Recurring Dream

B-SIDE
Instinct (live)
Distant Sun (live)
Fall At Your Feet (live)
Private Universe (live)
Fingers Of Love (live)
Better Be Home Soon (live)

RELEASED
24 June 1996 (album)
22 October 1996 (single)

RECORDED
1996

LABEL
Capitol

WRITER
Neil Finn

PRODUCERS
Mitchell Froom
Neil Finn
Tchad Blake

After the break-up of New Zealand's successful Split Enz in 1984, singer-songwriter Neil Finn and drummer Paul Hester formed Crowded House with bassist Nick Seymour and released their self-titled debut album in 1986. Finn's gift for writing irresistibly melodic songs such as 'Don't Dream It's Over' and 'Weather with You' secured the band a decade of hits and international success.

Sounding like a long-lost Lennon and McCartney number, the Beatles-influenced 'Not the Girl You Think You Are' is taken from Crowded House's first ever compilation album, 1996's *Recurring Dream: The Very Best of Crowded House*. This was the band's first No. 1 album in the UK and its third in Australia. It was the third new song to be released as a single from the album and reached No. 20 on the UK singles chart in 1996. Shortly after the single's release, the band played their final live show with the original line-up on 24 November outside the famous Sydney Opera House to an audience of over 120,000 people, recorded in the concert film and album *Farewell to the World*. Hester committed suicide in 2005 and the original members reformed a year later for the *Time on Earth* album.

⚡ PERFORMANCE TIPS

This is a somewhat muted song with unpredictable harmonies and a lilting waltz feel. The bass provides warm support with plenty of sustained notes, so make sure that the dotted minims last for the whole bar. There are also several moments where the bass adds melodic decoration, for example bars 14-17 and 39-45. Bring these sections out and be sure to capture the relaxed swing feel in the quavers.

NOT THE GIRL YOU THINK YOU ARE

WORDS AND MUSIC:
NEIL FINN

Verse

Swung Waltz ♩ = 94 (2 bars count-in)

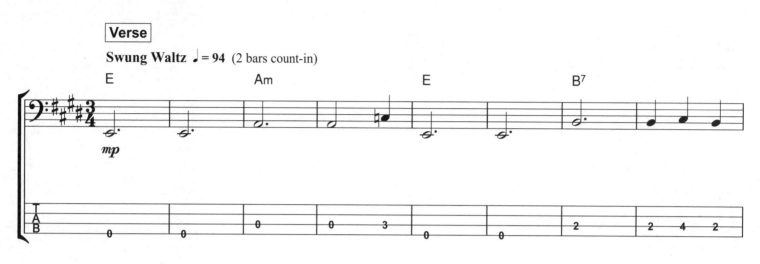

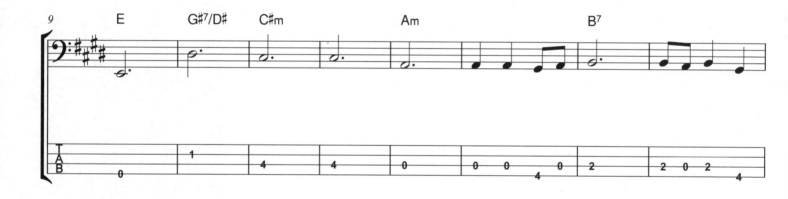

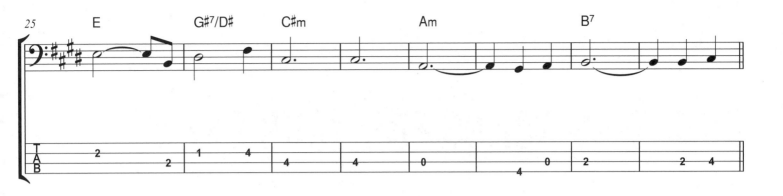

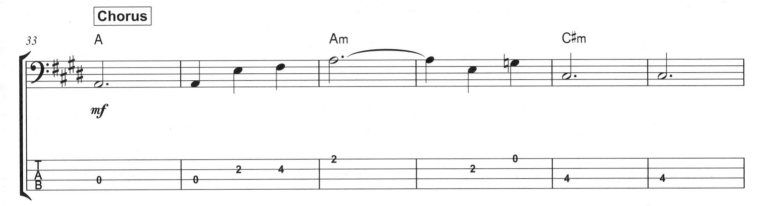

Chorus

CHOOSING SONGS FOR YOUR EXAM

SONG 1

Choose a song from this book.

SONG 2

Choose a song which is:

Either a different song from this book

or from the list of additional Trinity Rock & Pop arrangements, available at trinityrock.com

or from a printed or online source

or your own arrangement

or a song that you have written yourself

You can play Song 2 unaccompanied or with a backing track (minus the bass part). If you like, you can create a backing track yourself (or with friends), add your own vocals, or be accompanied live by another musician.

The level of difficulty and length of the song should be similar to the songs in this book and match the parameters available at trinityrock.com

When choosing a song, think about:

- Does it work on my instrument?

- Are there any technical elements that are too difficult for me? (If so, perhaps save it for when you do the next grade)

- Do I enjoy playing it?

- Does it work with my other songs to create a good set list?

SONG 3: TECHNICAL FOCUS

Song 3 is designed to help you develop specific and relevant techniques in performance. Choose one of the technical focus songs from this book, which cover two specific technical elements.

SHEET MUSIC

If your choice for Song 2 is not from this book, you must provide the examiner with a photocopy. The title, writers of the song and your name should be on the sheet music. You must also bring an original copy of the book, or a download version with proof of purchase, for each song that you perform in the exam.

Your music can be:

- A lead sheet with lyrics, chords and melody line

- A chord chart with lyrics

- A full score using conventional staff notation

PLAYING WITH BACKING TRACKS

All your backing tracks can be downloaded from soundwise.co.uk

- The backing tracks begin with a click track, which sets the tempo and helps you start accurately
- Be careful to balance the volume of the backing track against your instrument
- Listen carefully to the backing track to ensure that you are playing in time

If you are creating your own backing track, here are some further tips:

- Make sure that the sound quality is of a good standard
- Think carefully about the instruments/sounds you are using on the backing track
- Avoid copying what you are playing in the exam on the backing track – it should support, not duplicate
- Do you need to include a click track at the beginning?

COPYRIGHT IN A SONG

If you are a singer, instrumentalist or songwriter it is important to know about copyright. When someone writes a song they automatically own the copyright (sometimes called 'the rights'). Copyright begins once a piece of music has been documented or recorded (eg by video, CD or score notation) and protects the interests of the creators. This means that others cannot copy it, sell it, make it available online or record it without the owner's permission or the appropriate licence.

COVER VERSIONS

- When an artist creates a new version of a song it is called a 'cover version'
- The majority of songwriters subscribe to licensing agencies, also known as 'collecting societies'. When a songwriter is a member of such an agency, the performing rights to their material are transferred to the agency (this includes cover versions of their songs)
- The agency works on the writer's behalf by issuing licences to performance venues, who report what songs have been played, which in turn means that the songwriter will receive a payment for any songs used
- You can create a cover version of a song and use it in an exam without needing a licence

There are different rules for broadcasting (eg TV, radio, internet), selling or copying (pressing CDs, DVDs etc), and for printed material, and the appropriate licences should be sought out.

YOUR
PAGE
NOTES

YOUR
PAGE
NOTES

YOUR
PAGE
NOTES